The Terrible Life of a Beautiful Woman
The Blueprint for Self Love

AARON MALLORY

Thank you so much
for your support
Alishay!

ISBN: 0692954007
ISBN 13: 9780692954003

CONTENTS

FOREWORD: DAVID SHANDS

When Aaron first came to me looking for advice on how to build his brand, based on his philosophy and approach to the audience he was targeting, I honestly didn't think he would be able to capture or even attract the attention of the women that he wanted to help. His personality is very raw, straight forward and unapologetic. After a thirty minute conversation, I quickly realized that Aaron's biggest issue from a branding standpoint was not his message, but how he conveyed it. He's a great speaker on stage but writing a book is a little different. We both agreed that a lot of women would be receptive to solid, unfiltered perspectives from a male as long as it's done the right way. The success of this type of project may be very difficult for some people but Aaron had a totally different approach and I was excited to see how it come into fruition.

We all are in an age where social media has slightly changed the dynamic in how men and women deal with not only each other but our own personal identities. The genius in what Aaron has done in this book, that literally made me question my own tactics in relationships, is that he actually went and got help! He has truths that many women have never heard before, but he knew that without the help from women, those truths would possibly fall on deaf ears, or in this scenario, blind eyes. We men communicate a little differently than women so for Aaron to take the time to ask the opinions of different women was a great idea.

His original manuscript sounded like a man telling a woman what her issues are and how to fix them. This new work of art sounds like secrets that were told in confidence that only guys are privy to, but not only that, some of this information about women, most guys aren't aware of either. The "Terrible Life of a Beautiful Woman" is vulnerable, transparent, practical and extremely relatable. In every relationship that I've been in that ended unfavorably, it was never my fault; so I thought. Reading this book has honestly made me realize that I could have done a lot of things differently that would have given me, as well as the other person, more of an understanding of each other's point of view. The why's and the what's were so much more important than the faults of who. Your perceptions of simple as well as complicated situations will most likely evolve after putting this book down. I'm a better man because of it.

INTRODUCTION

I'm a heavily involved father of two beautiful daughters who are now both adults. Throughout their childhood, I spent time working to understand the opposite sex more in depth, in the hope that I might be able to see things as they did. My mother, God rest her soul, raised me to protect any woman I was around, so I became a self-proclaimed protector of women. I'm still a work in progress in my journey of learning, listening, and understanding. My goal in life is to promote unity in all people, regardless of race, sex, financial status, or religion, by showing individuals how others have the same needs and struggles.

1

CLARITY

A young girl is in the den. She is singing, dancing, and twirling around to the music coming from the living room, where her mother and two aunts are. Mom notices her singing and dancing with her eyes closed, feet sliding across the wood floor without a care in the world, and invites the girl's two aunts into the den to watch. Mom says, "Honey, we love it when you dance—you're such a free spirit." What happens when the girl notices that her loved ones are watching her dancing? She opens her eyes and immediately stops. Why does she stop? It's because she was *noticed*. Being noticed is actually a negative thing to our subconscious. When things and people in our lives move freely and independently, the act of noticing something could mean that something might be wrong or out of place. You are meant to move freely through this world and in your own mind. What I mean is, when you look in the mirror, don't overthink what you see. See you, and learn to love what you see; refrain from *noticing* every flaw. Overthinking or *noticing you* when nothing is even wrong should be looked at as unnatural. A bird doesn't notice that it's a bird unless it can no longer fly. Your body is your body, and you should appreciate it for simply running itself. As it does this internally, you should not notice it externally—unless, of course, something is wrong. The little girl was moving happily and freely across the floor and having a wonderful time, but when she was noticed doing this, she immediately became self-conscious. Her logic told her that she must be doing something wrong, embarrassing, or out of the ordinary for her mom and aunts to *notice*. In my own way of looking at the word *self-awareness*, I see it as something *internal*. *Self-consciousness*, on the other hand, is *external*. It's about being aware of your own appearance, actions, and thoughts versus being aware of *someone else being aware* of your appearance, actions, and thoughts. So doing something that is out of character for you, in order to be noticed by others, or simply noticing yourself being you can subconsciously be perceived as something being wrong or out of the ordinary, which might mean you won't be taken seriously. Be confident and sure of yourself, and you will stand out, because you are the only one noticing yourself every minute. I would like to change what you see when you look in the mirror every day. There will always be something you don't like on your body, but focus on bettering yourself as a person, because progression makes us all happy.

Writing this book has brought on so many different emotions, not only from me but also from everyone around me. The simple thought of this book comes with a lot of responsibility, actually more than I could have ever imagined. I had to sit back, look at this topic, and ask myself, "What result do I want to come from this?"

I envisioned sitting in front of someone's father and hearing him say, "What are your intentions with my daughter?" It's that important. My intentions must be put out on the table immediately. So here they are: my intent is to help women simply see things differently than they do now. It's that simple. What isn't simple is how I actually go about doing this.

As a man, I'm going to have to tread lightly while at the same time being real. You see, I don't have all the answers, nor am I claiming to. I'm not coming to you as some expert who claims he knows about women, and I'm not wanting to "fix" women either. If anyone needs fixing, it's men. I'll repeat that: if anyone needs fixing, *it's men*. There are a lot of lost, hurt, fatherless, angry men out here, and I look to serve you as your personal security advisor. Security advisor? Who am I to just throw myself into your life and appoint myself as something you aren't even sure you need? I've actually been raised to be a protector of women. Who raised me? A woman, of course—my beautiful mother, Carol Mallory.

2

DISPLACEMENT

My mom and I are from Philadelphia Pa, and after a nomadic series of events, we ended up in Atlanta Ga. For several reasons, my mom chose to leave Philly when I was about five years old. My dad was actually in my life at this particular age, but I lived with my Grandma Carrie, who was my dad's mother. Now the strange part of all of this is that I really have absolutely no recollection of spending time with my mother in Philly at all. The only memories I have are of my cousin Cahn, who would get dropped off at Grandma Carrie's house, and a few times of being with my dad. My dad was a little harsh with me at times—almost military-like. He would take Cahn and me jogging past the Liberty Bell Center. If we got tired, he would fuss. I didn't learn much from him, but I did learn at a young age to keep going without giving up. The only memory I have of my mom in Philly was when we were packing up our car to leave our hometown. She told me later that Philly had a lot of bad memories for her—her brother was murdered there, and her mother passed away in the same year. We moved to Syracuse, New York, and it was very cold, but I still had fun because I loved snow, and it snowed a lot. The snow would often actually be taller than me, which made it extremely fun to play in. I really enjoyed living there. I don't know what it was about the trees in Syracuse, but I may have climbed every tree in the neighborhood. For those who climbed trees as a child, it was awesome!

Mom attended the University of Syracuse, and she actually used to take me to school with her. Her classmates seemed to enjoy having me sit in the classroom with them. I would sit in the back and draw and color. During breaks, I would use my cuteness to ask the ladies for candy and gum. I can still remember the distinctive sound the act of digging in a purse made, with all of the various beauty-product containers clapping together as the nice women worked diligently to find a treat to give me. One night, I realized something that had never occurred to me before—just how precious and important my mom actually was to me. This realization was about to give me my first real feeling of loss. We were on the city bus heading home after picking up some groceries after class. It was a typical cold, snowy, dark evening, and our stop was coming up. She rang the bell on the bus to let the bus driver know that our stop was coming up, and we proceeded to the rear doors of the bus. For any of you who have never ridden a city bus (yes, there are people who have never ridden a bus before), the rear doors are pushed open by the passenger who is getting off; they aren't controlled by the bus driver. They also close after each passenger gets off, so when my mom got off first, the doors slammed shut in my face, and I fell back on the step. Before I knew it, the bus pulled off with me still on it! I was forced to watch the light of my life drift away into the darkness through the window. All I could see were her frightened face and hands reaching out to me and the bus. I was shocked at this point; all I could see was darkness outside. *She's gone! My mom is gone. What am I going to do?* What made things worse was that she had all the groceries! I only had a Kit Kat bar that the lady at the grocery store had handed me so I wouldn't have to search through the groceries to find it. How long could this Kit Kat bar last me before I starved to death? I started envisioning myself living under a bridge and saving the chocolate that was stuck to the wrapper for later. Then I snapped out of it and immediately started hollering and crying. Someone told the bus driver that I was still on the bus, and the driver stopped. It felt like time was going extremely slowly, because I was at the point where I had stopped crying, and the bus had stopped, but there was no indication that my mom was approaching the bus. I walked to the back of the bus, stood on a seat, and looked out the window. All I could see was darkness and snowflakes melting as they touched the glass. *What if she isn't coming? What if she slipped on some ice while she was chasing the bus?* Between her and me, my situation was OK at the moment, because I wasn't the one out in the dark, snowy, fifteen-degree weather. *What if she needs me instead of me needing her? What if she's getting mugged by someone because of all of the grocery bags?* The bus seemed like it took forever to simply come to a stop. Once it stopped, it seemed like we were already miles away from where my mom had gotten off. The waiting was horrific; I prayed to God to bring me my mom back, and I promised to keep her safe from that point on.

My mom finally caught up to the bus, and I was saved. It was very hard for me to let her out of my sight after that, and I could tell by the way she acted that the feeling was mutual. I knew that needed to get bigger. If I was bigger, I could have left the bus to go save her. My number-one objective was to get bigger after that ordeal; this five-year-old stuff was no longer working for me. Our bond became stronger after that eye-opening night, and to this day, this incident still pops into my mind almost every time I buy a Kit Kat bar at a grocery store.

As a little boy, I felt myself evolving into my mom's protector. In my mind, as that bus was pulling away, she was in more danger than I was, because of how cold and dark it was that night. I knew we had to protect each other. From that day forth, my mom was *my* responsibility, no matter how young I was. Later, we moved away from Syracuse to live with my aunt Yvonne, who lived in Raleigh, North Carolina. This was my first time meeting her, and we also began to bond with each other. Living with her was very temporary, because—you guessed it—we moved again. This time, we were heading to a city that I would fall in love with later in life and appreciate so much: Atlanta, Georgia. My aunt Rita told my mom that she had plenty of room for us to come live with her, so of course we came. Everything was great except for my aunt's pet dog. It was a *huge* Great Dane (Clifford the red dog was a Great Dane). This dog was my height on four legs, and I'm quite sure he weighed twice as much as I did. He used to jump on me almost every day, and even though he meant well, I was knocked down and actually felt bullied. Can you imagine being bullied by the family dog? I wasn't really happy living there and wished that we would move again. Whenever you make a wish, just keep in mind that *you may actually get what you wish for.* After telling my mom that it was OK for us to come and move in with her, my aunt asked us to leave because it turned out there wasn't enough room. This was when both of our lives were about to drastically change.

I noticed my mom being upset about us having to find somewhere else to go. To me, it seemed like moving was just something we did—we were nomads. I didn't have a problem with this at all, because we were leaving that freaking dog. Mom was always happy, but this time, she actually seemed worried. I immediately understood why. We didn't have anywhere to go this time, but before this move, it seemed like there had always been a plan. Not far from my aunt's house was a creepy motel called The Alamo—yes, it was as bad as it sounds. It was like a horror movie, but instead of zombies, there were drug addicts and prostitutes walking around all night. We were now officially homeless, and it was scary—very scary. It was horrible, but it was my job to protect my everything (my mom) from anything, so I had to put my fear to the side and be what I was raised to be. I would look at people with the evilest stare that I could give. We even saw someone get stabbed to death while we were on the way to the bus stop. I prayed that we would make it or move somewhere else quickly before I was the next one to get hurt for all of the mean stares I was giving people.

One day on the way back to the motel after getting off the bus, I stared a guy down with so much anger that I caused him to come toward us. While keeping a safe distance from my wrath, he told me that he wanted to congratulate me for protecting my mom by simply having the most unapproachable demeanor he'd ever seen a kid have and told me that the stares were actually working. It was like someone handed me a badge of honor. Apparently, the guy was a drug dealer who later made sure (or should I say helped me make sure) that no one messed with us. Our mini horror movie ended up coming to an end soon after that, because we found a homeless shelter that would take us. The place was pretty nice. It was a huge house with other displaced families living there, and we were a little safer. The shelter was right down the street from the Atlanta Zoo, so we would walk to it all the time, and this was when mom taught me how to always walk on the "traffic side" of her at all times as we walked to different places. My mom took this time to teach me how to grow into the role of protecting a woman. The first day she had me walk on the traffic side of her, she said, "A man's role is to protect and provide. Let me show you how to protect a woman. As you walk with any woman, you have to always be in a position to push the woman out of the way if a car was to veer off the road in our direction."

I remember looking around and asking, "So what would happen to me?"

She immediately stopped and kneeled in front of me and asked, "Would you rather I got hit by the car instead of you?"

I looked at her and said, "No, ma'am."

She went on to say, "A real man sacrifices everything in order to protect his family, including his own life. My safety is *your* responsibility, Aaron."

I looked at the most important person in my life and simply replied, "Yes, ma'am." After that, I would walk on the traffic side of her and dared a car to come our way. I grew up feeling this innate responsibility to protect any lady I was around.

We later finally found our very own apartment with no bullying dogs, no snow, no prostitutes, no drug addicts, and most important, no one to tell us that we were no longer welcome and had to leave. One or both of us could have really gotten hurt or possibly killed when we'd moved into that motel, and it gave me a feeling of only seeing my mom as my family; I never made a lot of effort to ask about or reach out to any other family members, including my dad. I was learning to be my own dad. I was the man of the house, and that's all that was needed.

When I was a year older, my mom started dating a guy who seemed very edgy to me. He talked with a lot of slang, and I would see him standing outside the neighborhood liquor store a lot when my mom sent me to the store. I didn't understand why or how my intelligent, well-spoken, strong queen of my life would date a "corner boy." That's what she would call her type one day when I asked her who that guy was to her. I was her little protector, and I didn't trust this guy. One summer night, I was awakened by strange, minute, scary noises. I lay there for a while but kept hearing them. I decided to get up to see what was going on. I walked down the hallway of our shotgun apartment—which meant that the hallway separated the living room and kitchen from the bedrooms and bathroom—to peek around the corner and see what the noise was. As I slowly looked around the corner into the living room, my heart dropped. I couldn't move; I was shocked. What I saw changed my life forever. My mom was being sexually abused on our living-room couch! The noise I was hearing was her trying to scream, but his huge hand was over her mouth, muffling her voice. My mom was crying. I had never seen my mom cry before. They noticed me standing there, and he removed his hand. She begged, "Please don't hurt my son."

I yelled out, *"Get off my mother!"*

She looked back at me with tears coming down the side of her face and said, "Aaron, go back to your room, and don't come out no matter what, do you hear me? Please don't hurt my son; please don't hurt my son...*go!*" I did as she said, and before I could lie down after closing my door, I heard the front door in the living room slam and my mom crying. I didn't come out of my room—I cried myself to sleep. Nothing was said about it the next day, and that guy never came back.

Years later, I actually saw this guy standing in line at the liquor store. I was about fourteen, and I was involved with a lot of negativity in my neighborhood at the time. I wanted to really hurt this guy, but I needed help. I told my friends who were with me that this guy had tried to rob me the other day, and I talked them into helping me jump him. There was a Dumpster behind the liquor store, so we went back there to look for some liquor bottles around to use as weapons. Back then, most bottles were made of glass instead of plastic. We found some and proceeded back to the front of the store. Then we walked inside and attacked him, hitting him in the head with the liquor bottles we had found. The bottle I was holding busted because I hit him so hard. He fell to the floor and looked back at me with a look that would make you think he was the most innocent person in the world. He had no idea who I was, he had no idea why he was being attacked, and he had no idea of the hurt he caused my mom and me. The owner of the store ran out from the back to run us off, but before I left this heartless rapist, I stood over him and said, "Don't you ever mistreat another woman ever again in life, because I'm watching you." I needed him to hear that, in case he thought that all of this was totally random. I was the self-proclaimed protector of women. I never saw him again, and my friends never knew the real story, because it wasn't their business. What was strange was that my mom continued to date the same type of guys—I didn't understand it. Why would she deal with the same type of dirtbag guys over and over again? When my mom did something that I perceived as self-destructive behavior, I began to realize that it might have had something to do with self-worth and how she viewed herself. It's possible that she was abused before the incident I happened to witness, and maybe, in some terrible way, it seemed "normal" to her. I realized I shouldn't judge. It wasn't really a problem because I was older now and fully capable of making sure that she was OK. A guy knows who to take advantage of and who not to mess with, especially a woman with a son who has a patented mean stare and newfound aggressive body language. I was my mother's protector. I started to see how habit, environment, and potential low self-esteem could have a woman feeling that it is OK to date "street guys"—or as my mom used to say, "corner boys"— even though they've shown abusive tendencies or lack of drive to better themselves. Nonetheless, my mom raised a man with the pride and servitude to uplift and adore any woman who blesses my life with her presence, because women are the reason we all are here to walk the earth in the first place. I am now the proud father of two beautiful young women who can confidently walk around with the knowledge that I'm only a phone call away any time they may need me. My mom passed away a few years after my youngest daughter was born. Her passing was one of the hardest things I've ever had to deal with in my life. I just hope she's still proud of me for upholding what she raised me to be.

My oldest daughter once called me at work, crying hysterically. I think she was twenty-two years old at the time. I immediately started walking to my car without even letting my boss know where I was going. By the time my daughter could tell me what was going on, I was already in my car, ready to beat somebody up. She told me that she had cut someone off in traffic on the way to her work, and the driver had apparently gotten so upset with her that he started following her. I told her to meet me near her job, hang up with me, and call the police. I was at her job almost as quickly as she was, ready to protect my baby. It turned out that the guy had stopped following her at some point when she was on the phone with the police. I gave her a big hug and made sure that she was OK mentally. This is who I am—I'm a man who takes pride in making the women in my life feel safe.

3

UNITY AND AWARENESS

So now that you know my story, how do I make *you* feel safe? You're just reading a book, right? Let's jump right in. The biggest part of feeling safe is awareness. Awareness of not only other people but your own actions. So what in the world does *The Terrible Life of a Beautiful Woman* have to do with any of this? *Unity, unity, unity.* I wish to present the thought of *uniting* with each other instead of competing, because so many of you are dealing with similar insecurities that are used to keep women separated systematically by the use of a weapon of mass destruction: *the mirror.* You see, society has the job of separating everyone from everyone else in hundreds of ways. Whether it be sexual preference, race, skin tone, nationality, weight, body type, religion, demographics, political affiliation, financial status, and so on. If I can enlighten you to the fact that nearly every other woman is dealing with or has dealt with the same battles of feeling inadequate, battling with self-esteem issues, or feeling in some way conditioned subconsciously to analyze and look for her flaws no matter who she is and how much money she has, you might begin to feel more comfortable in your own skin, which could lead to being comfortable being vulnerable around, meeting, and most importantly, *uniting* with women who may not think or look like you.

Every now and then, we all look at someone else and think, "Am I the only one feeling like this? Am I the only one going through as much?" Let me tell you a secret: *beautiful women have terrible lives.* It all depends on your perception of terrible, your perception of your own life, and the perception of the size of someone else's struggles compared to your own. The terrible part isn't the struggles; it's the pressure felt indirectly from other women who expect or assume a particular woman has a perfect life when she may possibly be going through more problems than anyone else but, for some reason, she holds the hurt in, smiles, and goes on as if things are great. The biggest culprits of this perceived terrible life are men, self-esteem, and time. Self-esteem issues are usually linked to either men or time. Some men can make the most beautiful woman feel like she simply isn't enough, she's losing her mind, or no one else would ever want her. Mix in time, which goes hand in hand with age, and a dash of no one to talk to, and there you go: a terrible life. My point of all this is that all people from all backgrounds go through things that can sometimes make us feel like we're inadequate. Communicating, spending time together, being vulnerable around each other, and no longer competing could change America, but this will not happen until women *collectively look at changing negative habits as a movement in order to better everyone.*

4

WHAT DOES LOVING YOURSELF REALLY MEAN?

When I hear a motivational speaker say, "Love yourself" to a crowd or on a video, I always think, *Is that enough?* Can someone take those words home with them and allow that thought to totally change their lives? Maybe, but there are people who need more than that simple statement, and for them, I would like to go deeper. It's so important to truly understand what these words mean in order for them to be properly worked into your everyday life. Everything we do that isn't automatic (like breathing, waking up, blinking, etc.) has to be done over and over again on purpose in order for it to turn into a habit. Loving yourself should be a habit, but before it can do that, it must first become a *belief.* How can you believe something you didn't believe before? You may not believe that you're pretty enough, you may not believe that you're good enough, and you may not believe that you're smart enough. But who is the person standing at this "enough bar" telling us who is and who isn't enough? Is it like being too short to ride a ride at a carnival? No, and do you realize that the word *enough* is the one thing that is in the way of you believing? You *are* enough, because there isn't a scale to tell you otherwise, and that's how you start believing. *You are enough!*

Next, we have to delve into the action of loving yourself to make it tangible and real. I think a lot of us feel that the saying isn't necessarily real and it sounds good to say, but it's just like loving someone else: if you can love your parents and your kids, you can easily love yourself too. One of the main reasons why we love our family members so much is because we've been through so much with them throughout the years and can't get rid of them. Another is that we believe we are supposed to love them. Many of us were never injected with the belief that we must love ourselves as we love family. But guess what? You're around yourself for years, and you can't get rid of yourself either, right? You wake up with yourself every morning, right? So love yourself. You still don't actually know how? It's OK. On we go.

When you love, you express patience and gratitude, you smile, you're happy, and your energy has a calmness when the person you love is around, because you feel safe and needed. But how do these feelings translate when who you love is yourself and you're not patient, you're not calm, and you don't make yourself feel safe? This is an example of how simply saying "love yourself" may not be enough a lot of the time. There are some things we all know about people, especially women—the mirror can be pretty hurtful; it shows all of our flaws, and we assume that others are looking at us as critically as we're looking at ourselves. The truth is, the mirror isn't showing you your flaws, your "radar" is. The number-one job your brain has is to use your senses to detect danger and protect your body from getting hurt in any way, just like the radar on a ship. Take for instance the radar guns that the state patrol uses. They have to set the speed that they want the radar gun to detect. If the trooper doesn't set the gun properly, the second he or she aims it at passing cars, it will go off at every car that passes. But as long as the trooper sets it to detect speeders going ninety miles per hour or above, the radar gun does its job. *Your own radar detector* (which is, of course, your brain) *is set way too high!* This brings us back to the word *belief.* If you believe yourself to have a face and body full of flaws, you'll have a face and body full of flaws. It's your brain; it's your belief; it's your radar. We all, including me, have issues with *something* involving ourselves. One of the reasons why we do this is because we are in some way judging ourselves or our situations against someone else or someone else's situations. The premise of this book is to show you that people have more *terrible lives* than you do, so comparing yourself to other people when you have no idea what is going on in the background of their lives is simply counterproductive in every way. I can't change your actions, but I can introduce a new habit or understanding to your life if you're open to it.

Loving yourself gets you prepared to love someone else, and the first step is to be thankful for what you *do have* and focus on what you *do want*. You see, we have a habit of focusing on what we don't have, don't want, and don't do. I'll give you an example. One time I was dating a very self-aware, intelligent woman, and she asked me what made me such a great catch. I went on to explain how I *don't* smoke weed or drink heavily, I *don't* cheat, I *don't* hang out all of the time, I *don't* try to control a woman when I'm in a relationship, I *don't* have family or baby-momma drama, and so on. She looked at me and said, "Is there a reason why you went on and on about what all you *don't* do instead of what you *do* do?" Until she pointed it out, I hadn't realized that was what I was doing. If you walk into a dark room that you've never been in, will you focus on what you *don't want* to happen or what you *do want* to happen? You *don't want* to stub your toe, you *don't want* to trip and fall, and you *don't want* to get hurt. It's all habit. But if you focus on *wanting* to find a light switch or a lamp, you'll find a way to light the dark room twice as fast. So loving yourself is all about focusing on what you have rather than what you don't have—when it pertains to your thoughts and intentions. If you go into an interview expecting the job and asking questions about where the company is going and how you can help them get there, you may just get the job. When you're that sure of yourself, the interviewer may begin to feel like you're the solution to his or her problem and you're ready to get to work. It will actually make the interviewer's job easier and more comfortable, because he or she might not have to recite the generic questions to you like he or she did with the other candidates. Instead, the interviewer will simply have a conversation with you and notice that you love yourself and are worth getting to know better.

Growing up, an average guy would easily admit that he doesn't necessarily understand women. To a certain degree, I'm in the same boat, but throughout the years, I'm proud to say that I've taken the time to learn from women by doing something guys don't usually do, which is *listen*. Why don't we as men usually listen? Because we don't utilize details the same way women do. The essence of a woman is simply *energy*. Energy can neither be created nor destroyed; it can only be transformed from one form to another. In other words, whatever you're going through doesn't go away; it just changes form, and that is where the main disconnect between men and women starts, and sadly, ends. That in itself can be frustrating, but your ongoing energy is needed because it has to be shared and transmitted to the people around you. Always remember, *you have been born with an ability that men do not possess*, the ability to bring another human being into existence. And because of this ability, you're wired differently than we are. A woman is responsible for the details of almost every situation, so your awareness of details is extremely high, and that is when overthinking often happens. This is when lack of trust for your decisions can cause you to lose love for yourself. You may get to a point where you just don't believe in yourself at all. Add in a guy who doesn't understand you, and you can really feel like you just want to crawl into a hole somewhere and hide. Even before having kids, women have a lot of responsibility, and it can be hard to not get down on yourself. Every adult woman is like the president of the United States in a way—you have all types of people needing your advice, judging your actions, wondering what you're doing, disapproving your decisions, questioning your credentials, and so on. But with all of that said, *they all would not be walking, talking, or breathing if you did not birth them. You are the beginning of life itself next to God!* Take your responsibility, your stress, and *your crown*, and hold your head high—*you are woman, you are beautiful, and you are a queen.* Start the habit of calling yourself a queen, start the habit of turning your "radar" down and appreciating how pretty you are without overanalyzing, and most importantly, start the habit of being selfish with your precious time and energy. Keep your cup full at all times. If you notice that it isn't full, fill it back up before you give a bit of it to anyone else. Never lose yourself in *anyone*, because you come first every day—if you aren't OK first and foremost, no one else will be. I hear women say that they love hard and they give relationships their all. My sister, *I want you to love yourself hard!* There are times when you must prove your love for yourself by revering yourself as the beginning, and with no beginning, there is nothing. Happiness and love is intrinsic, and *you are love*, so waiting for someone else to give it to you or make you happy can make that person the one main source of all of your emotions. That is not good at all, because if that person leaves, you'll be lost. *Lose yourself in yourself,* and start the habit of loving yourself.

5

FIVE MINUTES

Time

You've heard a million times, "Don't give it up too easily; make him wait for it; make him earn it." What is the *it* I'm speaking of? The *it* is *time*, you see—your body, your affection, your sex, and your heart are valuable, but these things may be valuable only to you. Another person may not value those things like you do, but *everyone* values time in some way. I want to steer you away from whether (or not) or when you have sex with someone to *how much of your valuable time* you allow someone to take from you.

Millions of people, male and female, have experienced the feeling that they've wasted a certain number of months or years being involved with someone and have wished that they could get that time back. Once something starts, like a relationship or a career, you can easily go too long or too far into it and not until later realize how much of yourself you've lost.

Whenever you meet someone, no matter who that person is, he or she will want a certain amount of time from you. That's the first objective, and anything else comes second. You have to ask yourself, "Is this person worth *five minutes* of my time?" Those five minutes, if not protected, can either enrich or ruin your entire life. Those five minutes are so precious because they open the door to so many things that may begin, continue, or end somewhere else. Just think about how much time you've wasted with your own life—you're OK with someone else wasting your time too? Have you ever been working on something very important and you decide to give five minutes to something else, like answering a call or text, looking at a post on social media, or looking at something interesting on television? Then you try to go back to the important task, and your focus is completely off. Your time is as precious as the air you breathe, and believe me, the air you breathe is more important than anything. How long will you stay in a room full of black smoke? No one would give even five minutes to that room.

Familiarity

Time changes the way you perceive something's value. Once something is extremely familiar because of long-term exposure, its value can get misconstrued to the point where it may become part of you, and leaving, removing, or stopping your exposure to it can be very difficult. It's almost like the entire thought process about whether to have sex or not is simply a decoy that takes your mind away from what's really important, because we look at sex as either on or off like a water faucet. There isn't a "how much" sex, you're either having it or you're not. If you want to have sex, have sex, but don't get hung up on the physical aspects. The bottom line is that sex doesn't get *wasted*; time does. Time affects everyone and everything; if you leave food out, it spoils, and if you eat it, you will most likely get sick. Even if food is in the refrigerator, time will still get to it. As you know, we as humans also have expiration dates, so we must use our time working on progressing and being happy.

Fear

A direct result of time and familiarity is *fear of the unknown*. Once you're used to something, somewhere, or someone, removing yourself from it may feel like getting off a drug. Your mind and body naturally adapt to whatever is going on, and at some point, your mind finds a way to justify why it isn't that bad and offers the thought that removing yourself from it could be worse than staying. The perception that something new may be worse than the bad situation you are in (we're assuming that this thing, person, or situation is not favorable) is the same feeling we discussed earlier when you pictured yourself in the dark room—you're focusing on what you *don't want* instead of what you *do want* again. You can sabotage your entire future when you don't allow yourself to evolve and grow by being open to what you want. Even if the new thing is bad, at least you overcame your fear of making a change.

Making mental assessments of what or who is taking up our time is the secret to any type of success. Remember, even as an adult, you're still growing as a person, so you may grow out of something, and it may be time for you to continue that growth by seeking new stimuli. The answer to any potential problem is a question. What am I still getting out of this? Should I move on? Is this really good for me? Is this person worth any more of my time? Will I die if I move on? What am I actually afraid of? Am I still growing? Is the other person still growing? Should I talk to someone about this?

Think about what I'm about to say long and hard, *every feeling we experience has to be justified for that feeling to stay*, and if you aren't conscious of this, your feelings will go in and out and up and down, and you'll push away the feelings instead of the person or situation. This can lead to being numb to situations or, on the other end of the spectrum, stressed and mad for no known reason. Part of loving yourself is being conscious of what is helping or allowing you to grow. We outgrow relationships, jobs, friends, habits, lifestyles, and even food (e.g., changing to a vegan lifestyle). Growth and progress make us happy, and that happiness comes deliberately. Don't be afraid to be happy.

I walk around happy every day, because I can easily justify why over and over again. But what happens when things go wrong in my life? I've been through so many things in my life, just as you have, where I seriously felt "God has me," and whatever I go through, I'm learning some sort of lesson or I'm part of someone else's lesson. In my opinion, everything happens for a reason, and whatever chain of events that may go on, it's simply a part of my growth or someone else's growth. I'm thankful and gracious for simply waking up this morning to see another day, and that, in turn, justifies my happiness and lack of fear of the unknown.

6

COMPETITION: KEYS DON'T COMPETE FOR LOCKS

Throughout this book, I'm covering a lot of topics, but the theme remains the same: loving yourself comes in a lot of different forms, and if you forget to put yourself first, you may once again lose yourself. This time we'll talk about losing yourself in competition. Sometimes we can get so deep into our feelings of wanting to "win" that we end up stressed and unhappy. My intent in life is to simply be happy—isn't that everyone's? But so many things can deter us from this goal. One of the biggest things, in my opinion, that holds a lot of us back is *perception*. Your perception of someone, something, or an event can make it seem totally different from what it may actually be. I read a book that taught me about two types of personalities—called warriors and architects—that compete with others in totally opposite ways. The warrior defeats, tears down, or intimidates others in order to win. In sports, one person or team must stop the other from scoring more points by the use of defense or hope that they fail in order to win. How many times have you seen players or fans of the opposing team almost pray that they miss a putt, a free throw, or a last-second field goal? We do this to others also, but instead of using defense, we may use insults, comments, looks, remarks, intimidation, or sarcasm to win. Architects, on the other hand, win not by tearing down, but by growing at a faster rate than others in some way. Some of us want to "win" so badly that we hurt others to the point where we end up hurting ourselves instead of building ourselves up to exactly where we want to be.

Arguments

You can't win an argument when the other person is left feeling wrong, belittled, or defeated. Winning an argument is like realizing that your tire is flat but continuing to drive to your destination anyway. You've gotten what you wanted, but you may have caused damage that may cost you something later. You're almost guaranteed at some point to lose the person that you keep winning arguments against. I believe in putting *wanting to be happy* over wanting to be right any day. Competing with your friend or mate in this way will slowly show them that they aren't as important as you are and may not be as smart as you are—and who wants to feel like that?

Infidelity

Ladies, never hold onto a man who cheats on you for the sake of *not wanting the other woman to win.* In the back of your mind, you may feel that if you leave, the other woman could come in, take your place, and go off into the sunset with the man you've built up to be a better man than he was when you met him. All of that hard work, just for her to come in, with no effort, to enjoy what you've built? *He cheated on you*, period. If you want to forgive him, fine, but don't stay with him because you don't want the other woman to "win." It's hard starting over, but that is sometimes what is needed. I want to enlighten you to something about men that you may not know: *we usually change our ways and evolve into better men in a woman's absence.* We learn our lessons by loss. What this means is that a loss can make a heavily flawed man wake up and snap out of it by discovering how much of a good thing he actually had in you, but now you're gone. Losing you could give him a feeling that he may never want to feel again. If you're considered irreplaceable in his eyes, he could realize what he truly has lost and either work hard to get you back or not allow a loss of this magnitude to happen again by cherishing what he has in the next woman. No one wants to build up a person that they havefallen in love with just to make that person better for someone else, but look at it this way: another woman could have done the same for the next guy you meet. It's a part of life. You may not be meant for that person; instead, you may have been meant to make that person better so he can be better for someone else. If a man doesn't treat you the way you want to be treated, let him go. Letting go is a learned behavior, and you must learn to do it over and over again. Just imagine having a habit of letting go of any man who doesn't treat you right—do you realize how powerful you would be? In the back of your head, you're probably thinking. "I can imagine how lonely I'd be," but having that habit would naturally attract better men, and you do know that if you change your habits, everything else will change too—it's all energy. This practice, if done by everyone, will make men and women better. This unselfish act of leaving and showing a man that you're not putting up with foolishness will make him better for his kids, his own life, the next woman, and the world, because you forced him to evolve. I have to add one more thing: you may be saving your own life too, because if you stay with him, he may feel like he could get away with anything and push your limits further and further. Loss is about learning, not defeat.

Other Women

To the women who do more (of anything) because they feel like other women are doing more, you could easily be causing yourself to look just like them and not be looked at as *special or unique*. We all enjoy feeling important, so just remember that everyone can't be important or special in the same way, because then you're the same as everyone else. Be yourself, and don't worry about what other women are doing. Being, walking, talking, looking, or acting like other women will cause you to be perceived as "replaceable." Just remember that different is attractive, and different is "irreplaceable." Have you ever heard someone say, "You are so special to me because you're just like every other woman I've ever been with"? Of course not. Love your hair, your nose, your legs, your feet, your stretch marks, your lips—love what makes you unique, and someone else will love those things too.

Imagine yourself as a key. You're unique for a reason. You're cut to fit into a lot of different locks, but you'll find out that most of these locks will not open. Certain keys seem like they fit, but you may never hear that *click*. You're looking for the click and not the fit—fitting is simply not enough. Keys are all cut differently and have flaws; those flaws are what make them special, and without those particular flaws, the lock the key was made for will never open.

7

PARTY FAVORS

In my opinion, this could be the most important chapter in this book. I'm specifically speaking to younger women here, and I would like to show you some things from a guy's point of view. A young woman gets to that age at which no one can tell her what to do, and there's a certain amount of carefree, unstressed energy about her. Depending on how things work out, she could be on top of the world. She's right for feeling like this—no matter how bad this sounds, a twenty-two-year-old woman could be the most desirable woman in the world. She's young, she may have not experienced a lot yet, she may not expect a lot of money or time to be spent on or with her, she most likely doesn't have the obligations an older woman may have, and most importantly, *she may not have been hurt yet*, so she may not have any walls up. After being hurt a few times, a man or woman naturally changes the way he or she approaches or receives someone.

The problem with this carefree age is that it could be a pivotal point in life where hurt, abuse, or—most scary of all—*love* can happen. In so many cases, young women are looked at as simply *party favors* by guys, and for that matter, by the rest of the world. So the young woman is sort of in the middle of getting a lot of the attention and not being taken seriously. Not being taken seriously isn't something you should be all right with, but until you've proven otherwise, you won't be. Get over the thought that you may not be valued, heard, or trusted by others. Have you ever received a friend request from someone on Facebook with no pictures or timeline? Would you accept or delete that request? That is how you are viewed by the world until people learn your character. This should be kept in mind when starting a new relationship. Go into it with the mind-set of "I'm just dating for practice, because I have to be honest with myself, I'm not really sure of what I want yet." This way, the chances of you getting hurt will be minimized. Don't worry about proving anything to the world, because it isn't time to do that. Just as others may not trust you, you shouldn't trust yourself yet either. Growth is about exposure and mistakes, but in the process of making those mistakes, it's imperative that you are aware of them and you make assessments of why and how the mistakes are made. You have to be the scientist in the lab and the lab mouse at the same time. The answer to any of your questions and problems will usually lie in the study of yourself while out in the world. Expose yourself to different things and people, and pay attention to how things make you feel and respond. This "I'm only a party favor at a party" mind-set will keep you aware of the thought that whoever is in front of you may not trust, understand, respect, or believe in you yet, and if that person says he or she does, can you believe it? Be at peace with the thought that he or she might be lying, and it's OK. There are thousands of women who can easily admit that they did something extremely irresponsible that may have changed their whole life and would label that time as when they were "young and dumb." This age range could be the biggest discovery stage since being a toddler—just learning how to walk, then talk, then draw, and so on. You're about to make a lot of mistakes, so have fun making them. As long as you learn from your surroundings, make assessments of the mistakes you make, and, no matter what, don't allow those assessments to cause you to overthink too much and get down on yourself. As long as you're growing and progressing by learning and understanding what's going on around you, that is an act of loving yourself. Remember to seek more, and this *more* that you seek is not going to care about you or respect you, because until you get older, you are just another party favor in the party.

8

WANTS VERSUS LIKES

This may seem like common sense, but the differences between these two words are so important to all of us, especially when it comes to the opposite sex.

- *Want*: something one desires to possess or wishes for. Examples: a house, a better life.
- *Like*: something one enjoys or feels pleasant about. Examples: a piece of candy, a sunny day.

As people move around their town or city, they run across people and things that they would like to experience. Sometimes the "like to experience" can be confused with a "want." I see Lamborghinis every now and then, and I think to myself, "one day," but in all honesty, I'm quite sure that if I ever bought one, the awkwardness of getting in and out of it and the cost to insure it—not to mention the sticker price—would possibly cause me to think, "I should have leased this thing," because it was more of a *like* instead of a *want*. I just wanted to enjoy or experience driving a Lamborghini around town for a while. We can look at each other the exact same way. Every day, we guys notice a fine, beautiful woman walk past and we like what we see, but some of us never take the time to think, "Do I *want* her or do I want to *experience* her?" You see, to want is to earn and qualify for, like a house. If you want a house, you have to *prepare your life for a house*. Your credit must be fairly good, your income must be adequate enough to sustain what will come with the house, like the mortgage payments and upkeep, and you may need to invest more money early on in the pursuit of obtaining this house. There may be others who are also interested, but do they want it as much as you do? This means that you'll have to wait for a decision to be made even after you've qualified, and you must be prepared to be committed to it. Now, in no way am I referring to people as cars or houses to be possessed, but these are simply examples to help move you along in the thought process.

Another way of thinking about *like versus want* is how we see candy. Many people have a favorite type of candy, but when we crave something sweet, just something sweet—anything sweet—will do. At certain times in our lives, we may run across someone that for whatever reason simply *will do*. Candy doesn't have to be qualified for or earned; there's no sacrifice or commitment to candy either, it's simply unwrapped and consumed. When you grow aware that you may be *liked* and not *wanted*, you now can keep a certain level of *detachment* throughout situations. I explain this to this degree because some women attract men because of what they think the man likes instead of what he wants. The girl who walks by wearing a tight, short dress may be what he *likes*, but the woman who just got off work or just left the gym may be what he *wants*. He may approach the girl with the short dress first—and that may be because it's easier to go after candy without a plan than a house without a plan. If a man approaches you without a plan, he may not see a house in front of him. So you may ask, "Aaron, what exactly does this having a plan look like?" It's simple. If a man approaches you with a hint of nervousness and a hint of confidence, a hint of humbleness and a hint of "I just have to meet you," and if the first time he has a chance to see you, he *plans a date* because he values the importance of a first impression, the effort will show you that he has thought things out. I'll share a harsh blanket statement with the young people: no one necessarily wants you until you have substance and business about yourself, so you must spend the time needed to earn the right to be looked at as a house and not candy—to be *wanted* instead of *liked*.

9

BE UNFORGIVING OF DOMESTIC VIOLENCE

I've had hundreds of conversations with women about this particular subject, and sometimes I find myself embarrassed by my fellow men who have hurt so many women in so many ways. Hitting a woman isn't justified ever. Me saying that I don't like the fact that one out of every five women you lay your eyes on has most likely been physically or sexually abused in some way isn't going to change anything. But I could possibly make one woman aware of how often this actually happens. I'll start by saying, *you are not alone*, and I know that it isn't easy to get out of abusive situations, but I want you to understand that if you don't work out a plan to somehow leave, you could lose your life.

As a man and a father of two grown daughters, I run the risk of one day going to jail simply because of the every fifth woman being abused probability. I don't condone violence, but I don't know what I would do if a guy were to put his hands on one of my little girls. There are a lot of men out here who think putting their hands on a woman is OK. That shows me that something is wrong with my fellow brothers. I don't care if you think you've found the perfect man, if he gives you any indication that he may have a temper, you let him go. If he actually puts his hands on you, *leave.* "How do I leave, Aaron? How? It's easy for you to say *leave* when you're sitting around, typing on a laptop. You aren't living this life, you don't know how this feels, and leaving isn't that easy! Where do I go? I don't have family here. We have kids together. If I leave, I would have to uproot my children from their schools!"

Call the Domestic Violence Hotline at 1-800-799-7233 or visit www. thehotline.org. Be careful going to any domestic violence help website at your home, because it could be monitored if you're on the house's Wi-Fi network. On your phone, Google "battered women's shelters in my area." Don't be afraid to seek help. I know it's scary, but take your kids and leave everything behind. Life is not going to be easy when you leave, but some of these situations end up with someone getting killed. It's better to be heavily inconvenienced for a while than to suffer another day of abuse. Leaving is twice as hard as staying because of the unknown. Another thing that may make it hard to leave is when the abuser apologizes and you really want to believe him. You may be waiting for him to change, or he may say things like, "You're the only woman who can evoke these feelings in me." Or, "I only get this angry because I love you so much." This may have you thinking that it's something that you're doing or not doing that may be causing him to hurt you.

If I can just:

- Make him happier...*no*, he has issues inside himself and those issues can lead to your death.
- Not get on his nerves so much...*no*, he put his hands on you, and it's time to move on.
- Stop messing up...*no*, no one deserves to be beaten because someone else is upset.
- Pay more attention to what I'm doing...*no*, it's not you; it's him, and it isn't your fault.

"But I don't want my family to look at me like I can't make good decisions. I've always put him on a pedestal; I'll be an embarrassment to everyone." You may die if you stay. Your family loves you, and it will be ok. Please allow your family to help.

Ask yourself two questions: Is staying loving myself, or is leaving loving myself? Make a decision that serves you.

From the day you meet a man to when you're married to him for ten years, he should not know where everyone in your family lives. If something were to happen, you'll have somewhere to go. Keep an account that he doesn't know about—this may violate some type of trust, but the fact is you must be able to leave home and possibly move away, which would mean quitting your job. It's sad that I have to say these things, but it is what it is. Domestic violence not only hurts the woman, but it also affects the children; I was one of those children it affected when my mom was sexually assaulted and abused. She taught me to protect her, and I took that responsibility seriously because of the abuse I had witnessed. I had an ex-girlfriend tell me that after we broke up, the guy she started dating beat her almost to death. To hear that someone I cared about started dating a guy who almost *killed her* was so hard for me. I've been asked a number of times why I don't focus on helping men instead of women. I feel like a lot of these guys have psychological issues, and I'm not a therapist. I'm here to help anyone I can help, but my mother raised me to protect women.

I have a true story to share with you. Names and details have been changed for obvious reasons. Teri and her husband, Torrence, had been married for only a year when things started to change in the dynamics of their relationship. The arguing was getting to a point where Teri simply was no longer happy. Her husband's actions during their arguments began to make her suspect that one day soon she might end up a victim of domestic violence. This particular situation was something I've never heard of *ever,* even in the movies. Teri and her husband were in their upstairs bathroom arguing. She was cleaning the bathtub and made a comment about how she wished he did a better job around the house helping her, since they both worked outside the home. Torrence replied that his ex-wife had never complained as much as she did. She got so upset that she took her ring off and threw it on the floor and told him that she no longer wanted to be with him. Given the title of this chapter, I'm sure you know what type of reply she got from him. He said that the only way she would leave him would be if she was taken out on a stretcher. She was shocked by his evil response and immediately tried to get up to put some clothes on in order to leave; he blocked her from leaving the bathroom and told her, "I guess you didn't hear me the first time." She sat back down and tried to regroup, now that she realized how serious this situation was. By the time Teri could go for her phone, he grabbed it and broke it across the corner of the bedroom dresser. Now she was really scared, so she started to plead with him to let her go. He asked her why she didn't want to be with him anymore, and instead of being calm, she got upset by the question and said she was tired of the constant arguing and was no longer happy. He got upset and unscrewed one of her perfume bottles, splattering it all over her and grabbing a lighter that she kept under the sink to light candles. He stood there looking at her. She was sitting on the edge of the bathtub in shock, crying, with perfume and tears dripping from her chin. What can anyone do in a situation like this?

She got fed up and yelled, *"Can I please leave?"* He flicked the lighter over and over again, as if to tease the thought of him actually using it on her. She asked him whether he actually thought these threats would make her change her feelings about an already-bad situation. Before she could do anything, he actually *lit her on fire!* She fell into the tub screaming and started to rip her nightgown off while still on fire. He panicked and grabbed a blanket from the bedroom, smothering the flames. She ran out of the bathroom and down the stairs as fast as she could, her husband started to realize the severity of what he had just done and didn't want her to go to the police so he chased her out of the house. She was running for her life down the street in her bra and panties with him on her heels, and she tripped and fell in the grass of someone's lawn. He then jumped on top of her, holding her partially burned body down and trying to reason with her in the hopes that she won't call the police.

The neighbor came outside with his firearm, demanded that Torrence get off Teri, and held him at gunpoint while his wife called the police. Teri got the help she needed at the hospital for the burns all over her body, and her husband went to prison.

I'm telling this story to let women know that things like this really happen—and not just on television. How do you avoid running into or dealing with men like this? *Run a full background check on any man who is serious about dating you.* Employers do it, so why shouldn't you? This would easily run the bad ones away. How do you ask a guy something like this? Simply say, "Hey, I just want you to know that I do background checks on guys because some guys out here are crazy, and I don't want to get stuck with that guy. If that creeps you out, I understand, but that's the only way I will get serious with someone." Research equals time, and time equals research. You can't catch everything, but being aware of how things progress and where they are progressing to is so important. The simple fact of you saying this to a guy sets a tone of no nonsense. People come into our lives for different reasons. Every guy you meet isn't meant to be your husband; it could be a great friendship instead. I would say that if you had male friends (who were actually only friends) and a potentially abusive guy knew this, he might think twice about dating you. When a man backs off for whatever reason, it could be a good thing without you even knowing it. Let him go if he wants to go, because you never know: you may have just dodged a bullet without knowing it. In conversation, tell a guy, "I'm a bullet dodger, and if I see anything off with a guy's behavior like abusive characteristics, I'm out, and the first thing I do is tell my guy friends what happened for extra support." This isn't guaranteed to work, but it sure would put seeds in a guy's mind. In my most humble opinion, it takes around two months to begin to see a guy's real self and another two months to see what a guy's real self actually wants. As Chris Rock said, you start off dating a person's representative. It's like going to a job interview. In most cases, you are your absolute best self on the interview, and once you're on the job, you're still learning your way around. But once the probation period is over and you can get insurance, only then does the real you start to peek out. After month number four, you're then comfortable enough to start complaining about management and thinking that you don't get paid enough. So that's about four months of consistently being around and "monitoring" someone to possibly show you who they are and what their issues may be. I always say that you don't know someone until something "stupid" happens and you get a chance to see how they react to the adversity. Now let me stop right there. I'm not talking about when you should have sex. I don't care when a woman decides to have sex, because as I mentioned in a previous chapter, giving someone your time is way more precious than whether you have sex or don't have sex with that person. Four months may be a long time to make a decision on whether you really say you know someone or not, but wouldn't you rather "monitor" someone for four months than waste ten years of your life with someone? In the monitoring stage, you take every opportunity to find out about him and your heart is on hold, because you can't give your heart to someone who can possibly be abusive.

For the women who have been abused, don't be too prideful to talk to someone before starting a new relationship. I strongly believe that if you're a broken person, you can easily attract another broken person without even knowing it. Imagine breaking your leg and instead of going to the doctor for a cast, you just continue to walk on it. What happens to your injury? It doesn't heal properly, and you continue to reinjure it over and over again to the point where it will never operate the same way again. Some of us need to put our hearts in a cast for a while, get help from a psychiatrist, and take the time to forgive the person who hurt us—not for that person's sake, but for our own peace of mind. You don't even have to talk to that person to forgive him—just forgive. Forgiving someone is the best way to let go of the regret and the memories. Your family and friends need you to move on from the past and focus on being happy again—no more sadness, no more resentment, no more pain.

10

THANK YOU FOR MAKING ME THE MAN I AM TODAY

Since the births of my daughters, I have felt the need to understand the differences in how women see and react to things compared to men. There are special women in all of our lives, but I would like to go further than verbally saying thank you—I would like to write a whole chapter saying it. I can literally write an entire book about how I've grown from who I've been around. If it wasn't for being exposed to these special individuals, I would not be the man I am today.

Carol
My mother, the reason not only for me being here but for me being me. She taught me how to appreciate what I do have instead of worrying about what I don't have, and most importantly she taught me how to treat a lady. I remember one time she taught me how to treat a lady who happened to be my downstairs neighbor. I saw her as the meanest old lady I'd ever met in my young life. My mom and I lived in these apartments called Highpoint Estates, and each apartment building had only four apartments, so they were shaped like large houses instead of the typical brick and concrete complexes. The staircase was wooden, and apparently the downstairs neighbors could hear everything when someone went up and

down the stairs. My friends used to come over my house because my mom was pretty cool with everyone being over; we would play video games, play rap music, and record ourselves rapping. Life was pretty good until we would leave to go outside. Every time we would run down the steps, mean ole Ms. Ida came out of her downstairs apartment yelling and cursing at us. I would talk to my mom about how I felt like I was being treated badly by Ms. Ida and how her words and tone was not only embarrassing but hurtful. My mom, the queen of my life, told me that her being mean was my own *perception*; she wasn't mean at all—*we were mean*. "Us? How on earth are we mean?" I asked. She asked me to put myself in her shoes and imagine how it would feel to be old and alone and all day long have to hear your upstairs neighbor's kid and his friends running up and down the hollow steps. She explained that when you're older, you begin to appreciate peace and quiet more, so we were likely simply interrupting her peace.

I asked my mom, "So what do I do to stop her from yelling at us? Crawl down the steps? I didn't build those steps. Should we put some sheets together and grapple out my window every time we leave the house?"

She said, "No, Aaron, just empathize with her. What this means is that you stop what you're doing to say that you understand how a group of boys running down the steps could be nerve-wracking, and you would do your best not to make so much noise." I was thinking that this wasn't going to work at all, and she said that I was right. I should catch her when she wasn't angry, like when I came home from school. She suggested that if I see her on the porch at that time of day, I should walk up to her and give her a hug.

"A hug? This lady hates me!" I said. She told me that if I think she hates me, it's my responsibility to make it right and talk about it. In one conversation, my mom taught me empathy, perception, communication, overcoming fear, and perspective. The next time I saw Ms. Ida, she was sweeping leaves off her front porch and I was coming home from school. I walked up to her, said, "Hey, Ms. Ida," and gave her a big hug. Then I told her exactly what my mom had told me to say. Believe it or not, she didn't kill me—she actually hugged me back! We talked, and after that day, I would sit with her and keep her company with the intent of simply making her smile. Ms. Ida later passed away, and I thanked my mom for teaching me empathy, because it gave me the chance to really get to know her, let her get to know me, and possibly added a little more happiness to her life. My mom—the queen of my life.

Tyler (My Oldest Daughter)

Tyler and I are totally alike and totally different all at the same time. We are both Pisces, and she actually had to break down what us being the same sign really meant in our relationship dynamic. One day, she actually sat me down and explained to me, "Daddy, you do know that the main reason why we butt heads all of the time is because we're the same sign, right?" I asked her what she meant. She replied, "Zodiac signs are real, and we both have a problem with authority." She was right—neither one of us like authority of any sort, and we are both dreamers, so as her dad, that's one strike on me simply for being her dad. I told her to have a plan; that's another strike against me, but the thing I've always seen is how she does right on her own, and that's all she wants me to see. If I tell her to do something, and then she does it and things turn out great, she might feel like she can't take credit for it, so she would rather do things on her own. She's twenty-four now, and I can still remember when she was seven years old and she noticed that I took a beer out the refrigerator and said to me, "Daddy, drinking beer isn't healthy, and you shouldn't drink it." To this day, I don't drink beer at all, mainly because I promised her that I wouldn't. To this day, we're either open to talk about *anything*, or we are beefing about something. I view her as a younger me. She actually is the person who got me to take a positive step in being a speaker. One day, she was invited to attend a free life-coach training class, and she wanted me to go with her. For whatever reason, the teacher enjoyed a point that I was making and asked me to elaborate. Even though I was sitting down, I felt like I had total control of a room full of strangers. That setting gave me the confidence I needed to take my talents to speak professionally. She did that—she put me in that setting. She is the reason I'm a speaker right now. We will always have this up and down relationship, though, and I'm used to it now. As I was writing this book, I would ask her opinion about certain chapters, and she would look at me and say, "No, Daddy, I don't like this chapter at all." I respect her opinion so much because one thing I know about her is that she holds nothing back, and we need that in our corners. We have a special bond that can never be broken; we've had discussions about everything and anything. She is my little me.

Kanesha (My Youngest Daughter)
Kanesha taught me twenty years ago that anything is possible. She almost didn't make it when she was a baby. She was very sickly and had to be on breathing machines at the hospital; her mom and I would just cry while looking at her little body hooked up to so many wires that we could barely see her chest. It was a scary time for us. We prayed and prayed that she would get better, only to have to take her to the hospital all over again. As her protector, I felt powerless, but she was the one who had the power, not me. She pulled through, and now I call her my little superhero. As she got older, she began to show the gift that she has to offer the world. She is a talented artist. She loved watching Pokémon and would pause the cartoon and draw each character before going back to watching the episode. She just completed her second year of college at SCAD, Savannah College of Art and Design. She has gotten straight As in school for the majority of her life, so it wasn't a surprise for her to tell me that she passed her second year with yet another A. She never gives up, no matter what obstacle is in front of her. It's just who she is. My little superhero.

Efie
She is the beautiful mother of my children, and she's so much more than that. Efie is my friend; our marriage may have ended, but the bond that we have as parents is just as special. There's a phrase that people usually use with their children, but I have *unconditional love* for her as well as my daughters. We've been through so much as a family that I would give her one of my lungs if she needed it. I was only nineteen when we met, fell in love, and started a family. Because of how young we were, we weren't able to survive the ups and downs of marriage. It ended, but our passion and goal of raising these little girls to be great women didn't. We would get on

the phone and talk about our kids like a CEO and CFO talk about their company in a boardroom. Our girls saw that and felt it too—we were so involved. And even now that our girls are grown, they know how much we stay on them. They need us differently now, but they still need us in their own way. When our girls were little and had a problem with a boy picking on them at school, Efie would ask, "Do you want Daddy to get 'em?" They would usually say yes, and she would call me, and I would stop whatever it was I was doing and go up to the school that day to find out *who was messing with my little girl*. One time, Tyler had a problem with a boy in middle school, and he left before I could get there because school had just let out. Efie asked one of the other kids where the boy lived and what kind of car the parent drove. We rode up and down the street where the boy lived in order to knock on their door to talk to the parents, but we didn't see the car. Of course, I was right back up at the school the next day to talk to the principal. We were "ride or die" parents for real. The other kids saw just how passionate Tyler's parents were about making sure she was OK; she didn't have any other problems for the rest of her time there. One day during the 2008 recession, I lost my job. I'd never lost a job before, so I was worried and frustrated, mainly because so many other people lost their jobs at the same time as I did, which meant there were more jobless candidates than job openings. I called Efie to vent and give her my valid excuse on why I didn't have any money and couldn't find a job. She stopped my words and said, "Aaron, our kids can't eat excuses; do something about this now!" She sounded like the wife of Denzel Washington in the movie *John Q* when she told him to "Do something!" A man needs that, and I started looking for work outside of Atlanta and eventually found work about 150 miles away in the city of Columbus, Georgia. I took the job and was able to get my life back on track, and Columbus was pretty cool too.

Efie also actually started me off with book writing, because she was in the process of writing her own book about her life, and she wanted me to write the chapter involving our marriage. I didn't really know what to write, so I simply wrote from my memories. Before I knew it, I had written ten pages in an hour. I sat there looking at those pages and said, "Wow, I can write a book!" She inspired me to simply start writing, and that was what I did. Married or not married, every man needs a woman like that in his corner.

Antoinette

After working at my new job in Columbus for a while, I began to get comfortable enough to start dating again, and I met Antoinette. She seemed to be the sweetest woman I'd ever met in my whole life, and what I didn't know was that she was about to change that life of mine forever. I met her in line at the Dollar Store. She was slim with fairly long hair, and she had big, beautiful eyes. We talked, exchanged phone numbers, talked for a while, and eventually we started dating. Early on, she told me that she had lupus, but I had an extended family member who also had it, and she had her issues here and there but was OK overall. We got close pretty fast, because she told me that she had a stalker who was apparently an ex who didn't want to let go. She was so bothered by this guy that simply explaining the situation to me made tears come to her eyes. I told her to give me his phone number, and every time he called or texted her, I would call or text him the exact thing he was texting her. He got freaked out by what was happening, and he just ended up leaving her alone. She had two kids, a son and a beautiful daughter. Her daughter was seven, and her son was twelve at the time. I'll never forget how her son mean mugged me the first time I came to their house. I totally understood why—he was the man of the house, and I was an intruder; he was the protector of his mom and his sister. After some time, he got cool with his mom and me dating, and actually we got to the point where we were outside throwing the football around together. Antoinette's kids' father was active in their lives and was a pretty cool guy. He appreciated me throwing the football around with his son, and I was appreciative of the fact that there was no drama or issues with anyone. I got to know other members of her family, and things were going well, until she lost her job and she started getting depressed. Now, I knew exactly how she felt, because something similar had happened to me, so I was on her like my kids' mom was on me, but for whatever reason, she didn't react like I did. Instead, my pushing her to keep trying to look for work was a major problem for her. She began to want to be by herself, and I actually was OK with that, because she became a different person. Her not wanting me to help in any way, or even be around for that matter, kept our budding relationship from growing. I have a personal rule that I go by: you never know someone until some type of adversity happens. Her being down on herself made me down, and I was still trying to get up myself. The energy was just so different, and I felt pushed away inadvertently. I couldn't compare her situation to mine, but the lack of effort in doing anything started making me feel a certain way. I still checked on her to see if she needed anything, and one day I found out that she was getting sick. Things started to change, and after a certain amount of time, she was in and out of the hospital so often that it began to seem normal. She eventually started losing weight, and then her hair, and finally she wound up in a wheelchair. I was afraid for her. Once again, I felt powerless, and I wasn't able to protect her.

I was working a night job, and I would get off at seven o'clock in the morning. I received a text from Antoinette's aunt telling me to come to the hospital when I got off. I figured she must have needed some help with getting her home as usual. I got off and drove to the hospital, and when I pulled up to the entrance, the whole family was standing outside. My eyes started filling up with tears. I sat there for a second before I got out of the car. The first person to greet me was her kids' father, who told me that she had passed away an hour ago. We all hugged and said a prayer. The kids' eyes were red from crying as I hugged them. Antoinette taught me a valuable lesson: don't take anything or anyone for granted. If you have an argument or a fallout with someone, apologize and hug that person, even if they were wrong; a life can end in a minute, and nothing is promised to any of us. You never know what someone is going through. Don't give us our flowers when it's too late. *I want my flowers now, I want my hug now, I want my happiness while I'm still on this earth, and I want to enjoy my life now.* She was only twenty-eight years young. My mom didn't work my whole life, and when I viewed her not wanting to work, it reminded me of my mom, and I was fine with backing off. I should have stayed with her instead of giving up so easily. She was going through things that I didn't know about; she needed me, and I wasn't there like I should have been. I wanted to push her to get another job, but that was what I wanted and not what *she needed*, which might have been for me just to be silent and there next to her instead of trying to fix the situation. People don't need solutions or to be fixed all the time. Sometimes they simply need compassion and a comforting hand to hold. I miss you, Antoinette.

I recently went to her son's high-school graduation and was able to hang out with the family afterward. It was good to see everyone. His father and I laughed at how one day Antoinette called him over to her house when I was there and told him, "This is the man who will be around your kids, so I'll leave out so y'all can get acquainted." She walked outside as we just sat there and awkwardly small talked but soon ended up being good friends after that. We all had a good time talking about our special memories of her. I later sat her son down to show him what I'd written in this book about her. He read it and gave me his blessing. I chose the color purple on the front of this book to raise awareness for lupus.

Bianca

I met this amazing soul at the night job I was working at in Columbus. She worked in the office while everyone else worked downstairs in the factory. Bianca was a hardworking, positive person who always had a smile on her face, even when there were rumors of layoffs at the plant. I ended up leaving this job to finally move back to Atlanta, and Bianca and I always kept in touch after I left. One day, she called me and told me that she had breast cancer. She wasn't crying, and she didn't sound worried. She just said, "They could cut these things off as far as I'm concerned." She understood that this ordeal was going to be a process—she was ready to go to war with cancer, and she had no choice but to be ready. I would periodically call to check on her, and she would be tired, nauseated, and exhausted from the Thursday treatments she was receiving, but there was never a note of defeat in her voice at all. As time went by, I would see her on Facebook at different hospitals taking selfies with other cancer patients with the biggest smile imaginable. She lost her hair and would just throw a hat on and keep smiling and inspiring with her amazing positivity, doing cancer walks and helping everyone whenever she could. After less than six months of treatment, she had surgery and *beat cancer!* After winning this war, she looked at her life, stopped working so much, and started living. The next thing I knew, there was Bianca on Facebook with all green on with beads around her neck in New Orleans celebrating St. Patrick's Day, looking like she was having a ball with that same joyful smile! She reinforced what my mom always taught me when I was growing up: *smile through adversity from beginning to end.* Life is 20 percent what happens to you and 80 percent how you respond to it—*attitude, attitude, attitude.* Thank you, Bianca, for reminding me to smile!

Tonya

Simply knowing Tonya is an example of "everything happens for a reason." I'll get to that later. This woman may only be five foot two, but she stands in the face of adversity like she's six feet tall. She was dealing with some past issues when I first met her. I was single at the time and thought she was so beautiful, but with everything she had just been through with her ex-husband, she stayed a little distant. Still, she was so intriguing to me as a person that I wanted to get to know her and simply be friends. As time went by, she divulged her past issues to me. She had been physically abused by her ex-husband, and she was actually, for loss of a better word, running from him. He didn't know where she had moved to, and she didn't trust anyone else to know either. These guys, man—I just don't understand how men do this. We ended up being good friends, as we both had common writing and social-media interests. In fact, she actually introduced me to how Instagram can be used to put yourself out there more. Fast forward five months, and she was on the fence about leaving her dead-end job that she hated to go to a better job that was twice as far to get to. She wanted to know what I would do if I were in her position. I easily said to her to take risks in life and go for it. She started the new job and loved it, but of course there's a but—after less than a month of working there, she got laid off. Now, when you get laid off after just starting a job, you aren't eligible to receive unemployment compensation and you're left with no insurance. She had two young children, a girl and a boy. The boy had very bad asthma, which would add to the stress that was on her already. One day, I texted this extremely resilient woman to see how she was doing and she texted back a crying emoji. Now, I learned from what happened with Antoinette, when I got all motivational drill sergeant with her, that I can't be like that with everyone, so I held back a little and called her to ask if things were getting way too frustrating or did something else happen. She said something else had happened and she'd tell me what it was when she was ready. I was thinking maybe her ex-husband had found where she lived or something. She told me that she had stage 3 ovarian cancer. I looked at the text and replied quickly. She was shocked by my reply. "Cancer is weak these days; focus on the job situation and not that. After a few crappy months, you'll beat it, and you'll be fine." I was sending Bianca's strength straight to Tonya—this woman had just lost her job after leaving a job she was comfortable at, and now she found out that she had cancer? I'm sorry, *stage 3* cancer? I knew I had to keep this woman strong. How do you get proper cancer treatment when you don't have insurance, though? When you believe that there's a way, God makes a way—you just have to want it and ask for it. Somehow, she was able to get state funding to pay for her treatments. This is where the will to win comes in—she didn't get down on herself, kept looking for work, and started treatment. I wasn't worried at all, especially if she wasn't worried—let's get it!

This is a true story, so what I'm about to write may sound made up, but the truth is she had surgery to remove all of the cancer and found a job—all within two weeks! I wasn't worried about her at all, but I would never have imagined her beating cancer this freaking fast! Now she's cancer-free, has a new job, and has a new perspective on life. What else can I say but God is good?

Lisa

This woman is a ball of fire rolling down a steep hill. For years, Lisa has been a full-time, successful entrepreneur, and I appreciate the energy she gives to this world. That energy is enough to run a nuclear reactor. She's so excited about life that she would admit that she has trouble sleeping because she's so excited about the next day. I was working on this book when I met her. We knew the same people, and I ended up running across her

Instagram page. She had some model-type shots, and I reached out to her to see if I could possibly pay her for one of her pictures to be on the cover of my book. The first time we talked, I think we talked for over an hour. I agreed to send her what I'd written so far, and every time we talked, it was hard to end the conversation. After reading what I sent her, she told me that for my book to fit her brand, I had to lighten up the tone of the book, because it came off as too harsh. Between me sending her my chapters and her reading them, we talked enough for her to feel invested to the point where she felt comfortable to say this. I'm sure in any other situation, a simple "sorry, but I'm not interested" would have sufficed. Her suggesting that I rewrite my book was bold enough for me to take notice and ask more questions. As time went by, I learned so many more perspectives and nuances about women from different women. Certain things like learning about a woman's pain would have me intrigued, and I realized that I simply wasn't asking the right questions when I had initially done my research. I realized that what I had already written was only touching the surface of what I wanted to accomplish. This book really could change lives. I literally started from scratch and wrote the entire book over. Lisa and I were at a point where we were in contact with each other almost every day, talking about actively intending on changing the world. Something I realized by talking with Lisa was that men and women may not befriend each other as much as they should. For that matter, I would also say the same thing about women befriending other women who aren't necessarily in their circle. I decided to go in another direction with the book cover, but I gained a great friend and a totally new perspective and respect for how important every woman is to this world.

The women in this chapter and others are not only a part of my story, but they've played a major part in my evolution as a man. I am a better man because of you. Thank you all.

11

A WOMAN'S PAIN
(LIKE I ACTUALLY KNOW)

I've had a lot of conversations with a number of women about a lot of different things. One day, I asked a friend of mine, "What are the biggest issues women have?"

She replied, "Men! Are you kidding me? Aaron, you don't understand a woman's pain."

I replied, "A woman's pain? Can you elaborate? What do you mean?"

Safety is something that is on a woman's mind virtually every day. A woman is on defense in some way whenever she's out because of us men. She can't even walk down the street in broad daylight without the thought of in some way needing to protect herself. She has to watch her back at all times, especially when she's out at night. Just the normal act of getting off work late can sometimes be a movie clip—walking through a dark parking deck with her keys in her hand, and all that is heard is the echo of her heels hitting the pavement. Then she hears a faint clicking noise over in the darkness; she hurries to her car, closes the door, and drives away. We as men don't have to worry about some creepy woman jumping out of the bushes trying to sexually assault or mug us. One woman I spoke to actually said that the world would be a better place if there were no men at all. Just hearing someone say that really hurt. She said that the men are the ones who do the majority of the crimes in the world. We seriously have to do better as men as a whole.

Being judged by other women from head to toe and creepy guys making you feel uncomfortable can really interrupt your flow as you move through your day. Maintaining positive energy can be difficult when every time you walk into a room, you have women, as well as men, staring at you for totally different reasons. A friend of mine also said that simply breaking up with a guy can be scary because there's always the possibility that he could turn into an "If I can't have you, no one can" stalker.

Abuse is worse than safety, because it usually happens in a woman's own home. After it happens and the woman leaves or survives, in many cases she may have problems trusting again. Abuse isn't always physical; it can be mental, and sometimes mental can be worse. We as men may never deal with abuse of any kind the same way a woman does. I know that there are men who suffer from certain forms of abuse, but it is not the same.

Going into job interviews can be a totally different experience for women. I once knew a woman who was heading to an interview and, of course, I said to her, "You'll do great; just go in there with confidence."

She replied, "Well, I don't want to come off as too confident, because whether it's a male or female interviewer, I may come off as bossy." I was thinking, *Wow.* What a perfect example of *The Terrible Life of a Beautiful Woman.* A beautiful woman may get the job or not, simply because of how she looks and not by her own merit. She can actually be viewed as a threat to someone presently working there.

Fitting into clothes can be a huge issue for women. A top may fit, but the rest may not because of her shape. A woman might try on ten outfits and still not be able to find one that fits her properly. This is where self-esteem issues come into play. A woman's body changes a lot more than a man's body does over time.

Raising children is a beautiful thing, but it can get very difficult, especially when a woman has to do it on her own. She is usually the custodial parent during a breakup or divorce, so while she's full of hurt and regret and may just want to sit alone and cry, guess what? She has a household to hold together so *there may not be any time to cry.* She has to put her wants, her needs, and her "me time" all aside in order to wake the kids up, bathe them, clothe them, feed them, and take them to school. When she gets off work, she can't simply go home. She has to pick the kids up, ask them how their day was, stop at the grocery store, make sure she doesn't let them out of her sight, go home to cook, read them a bedtime story, and argue with them while they make up excuses to stay up ten more minutes. By that time, she's dead tired and goes to bed just to do it all over again. I salute the mothers. Thank you for all that you do, because I know it's not easy. A woman's commitment is real, a woman's loyalty is real, and a woman's pain is real. Again, thank you for everything you do.

12

PERMISSION

Sit back with a glass of wine, play some soothing music, and recite these corresponding words aloud to yourself while expressing what each statement means to you. This is a way of releasing all of the things that are keeping you from being great. You never know; you could find yourself beginning to write your own book inside of this book. A paragraph can turn into a page, and a few pages can turn into a book. I'm leaving you some blank pages for you to get started on your own story. Thank you for going through these emotions and this journey with me. This was my life in its most vulnerable form.

I HAVE PERMISSION TO BE
MYSELF

I HAVE PERMISSION TO BE HAPPY

I HAVE PERMISSION TO BE VULNERABLE

I HAVE PERMISSION TO BE CONFIDENT

I HAVE PERMISSION TO NO LONGER SECOND-GUESS MYSELF

I HAVE PERMISSION TO SMILE

I HAVE PERMISSION TO TRUST AGAIN

I HAVE PERMISSION TO ERASE MY EX'S TEXT THREAD

I HAVE PERMISSION TO LEAVE

I HAVE PERMISSION TO LOVE AGAIN

I HAVE PERMISSION TO LET GO OF MY PAST

I HAVE PERMISSION TO CUT OFF
PEOPLE WHO DON'T SERVE MY
BEST INTERESTS

I HAVE PERMISSION TO CRY

I HAVE PERMISSION TO BE DIFFERENT

I HAVE PERMISSION TO STEP OUTSIDE OF MY COMFORT ZONE

I HAVE PERMISSION TO PUT MYSELF FIRST

I HAVE PERMISSION TO LET GO
OF MY INDEPENDENCE

I HAVE PERMISSION TO LOVE
MYSELF BECAUSE I NOW KNOW
WHAT THAT LOOKS LIKE